geography

edward dorn

geography

fulcrum press london

acknowledgements

Some of these poems first appeared in
Coyote's Journal, El Corno Emplumado, Fubbalo, Granta,
Matter, The Nation, Niagara Frontier Review, Northwest
Review, Paris Review, Peace News, Prospect, and Wild
Dog. *Idaho Out* was also published with a preface by the
author Fulcrum Press 1965. This March Afternoon,
Daffodil Song, and Dark Ceiling first appeared in Poetry.
The cover design is by Fielding Dawson. The typography is
by Stuart Montgomery. Printed in Great Britain by Villiers
Publications Ltd London NW5 for Fulcrum Press 20 Fitzroy
Sq. London W1. Distributed in USA by Horizon Press
156 Fifth Ave. New York NY 10010.

contents

geography

for charles olson

SONG: THE ASTRONAUTS

for clair oursler

On the bed of the vast promiscuity
of the poet's senses is turned
the multiple world, no love is possible
that has not received the
freight of that fact
no wake permissible that has not met
the fluxes of those oceans.
the moon orbits
only for that permission.
Men with fine bones in their heads
will manipulate a recovery
and put spades into her
only to find Euripides went before them
            the hymen long ago fixed
it is an old old wedding
but as you dig you will not hear
the marriage flutes
you will be killed in your sleep.
Broken.
you will be considered pirates
and killed when Hymenaeus
(who lost his voice and life
            singing at a wedding
catches you asleep
in the rushes of
the windless moon

        the immensely soft glow of it
        will always be behind you
        as you stand on its face
                staring
            at the strangely
        inhabited world
                from whence you came
        from where all men with their eyes
        have been satisfied

            before thee

9

THE PROBLEM OF THE POEM FOR MY DAUGHTER, LEFT UNSOLVED

The darkness rings.
                    the surface form
          of the face, a halo
of the face,
as it passes away in the air as she moves
    between the buildings, a cut
    surrounding her throat, the pearls
    of the price she'll never have to insist
she paid
          a thin line red with its own distinction
some goiter
of what she has been made to understand is civilization
not the brand of the adventurous cutlass

The misery is superficial now.
I have dwelt on that quality in other poems
without attention to the obvious
drain
          of social definition
the oblivious process
of a brutal economic calculus, where to
                              place the dark hair
save above moist eyes
the black slacks,
the desperately optimistic rouge of the fallen cheeks
                              (cheeks are up
when they live
          both forward *and*
posterior, the colorado of new day not a new state . . .
where the leads are I despair to find lead mines

                    In the chronically vast complex
explanation, a field true,
but a field
no field hand knows
beyond the produce of it
          on some citizen's land, the horizons
sheer the top
    of the head of the man
        who is bent

        bent is an attitude
    I've settled on now
        to define a man
    whose attention is forced down
a class, distracted, not a stratum
detained from what the reaper called attention
        might harvest, O false shift of season
in a vacation
                but how slow, and seasonal
        and the poem is an instrument of intellection
        thus a condition
        of the simultaneous
        so the woman and myself, pass,
        and her message bears a huge meanness
                "the measureless crudity of the States"

A world where no thing thrives short of the total pestilence
of its spirit, and because there is no intelligence short
of the total there is no intelligence, none. There is not even one
intelligence in the land, children see the capitol of things
shifted to disneyland, no misery
which does not know all misery,
as an eye of knowledge, contrary to happiness
that quite exclusive short range and burst, as it happens
a birthday party, my daughter's. I had gone to the supermarket
for ice cream.   and saw the shocked woman

        We call the intersection of time
and event the
devastation of a fortune cake
all answers pulled out
of the standard of living which is that cake
no standard is cake
a provided nation
is no standard, rather a thorn
in the side of a more careful world
        her pain affirmed (all men and women
who suffer deeply, in any way, are not
cannot be U.S. Citizens, no matter where
they live. They may live in Indiana
        she carried no standard,
        as I saw her: impossible to be a citizen
        there is no such thing anywhere, in any country.
    I could have shot her down, had she been a marine.
She was a housewife.

11

And leaving the scene, and the legal questions
not one male canaanite would have come forward
She was no phœnician raped broad,
there are never any ships parked by the bannock county court house
this woman was sometime willingly captured by another,
a sort of community, her husband, if she is unfortunate enough to

possess one

is probably a masonic reservist.

No woman is Helena
unless the culture has provided for the passage of pain
and no people can construct the delicacies of culture
until they imagine Helena, merely fucking in the middle
of the atlantic on the SS United States is not it, is procurement
while the full-sized poodle whines in the kennel above
back of the forward stack, the echo of the sound he makes in Berkeley
where the hippest member of the minority group as it was reported
arrived in a sports car and there it was, white, with a beret
wearing shades, sitting beside the driver, looking with disdain
on a small cur who trotted along the curb and stopped
for one brief moment of curiosity and then resumed
his policing of the bases of parking meters

These United States.
have sent forth women, hopeless divorcees,
the wrinkled millionairesses of resources dwindled
to a day dream, the exhausted mesaba of their dangling breasts
soft wax structures to support our collectively ceaseless greed
for legitimate youth, but divided states do not create women,
Amelia Earhart
was not carried off, she flew, like something familiarly
transvestite in us, a weirdly technical Icarus
she was sent for by some morse-code spiritism, this land
was never more than the bitter hardness of nouns for us
her destiny was not qualified by myth

She came in all her beauty
to a small green island
in a bag of metal, oh misfortune that to be exemplary is so difficult
she could have been a goddess because she flew, other women
marked by sex, fold out of the minds of american men
who may no longer wear the bottoms of their trousers rolled
but who are certainly all circumcised without ritual
and wear the ends of their penises rolled
and always assure their dentists they are masturbators :

                                                        the paraphernalia
of an existence, thus a human phenomenon, culture-less
(pop culture,
                technologically provisioned
(those are collections of people grasping nothing
                                        the women are
                        set loose to walk spiritless
their marks are deep cuts on the neck, moist eyes, sagging nylons
eyes painted to dry everything, loose figures of despair
or hard flesh prolonged by injections and tucks into an isolated youngness
a manufactured Galateability
                                The end
                                of applied genetics will be
                                the elimination of freely disposed
                                intellection, via the rule
                                that a science is oriented toward
                                        Use, some predictable
                        breed, is the end
(Automation ends with a moral proposition, THE LESSON of
one maximum factor of it
will suggest all the correspondences:
                                mail food ads
                                the attractive stuffing
                                from McCalls and House Beautiful
                                to Havana
                                        during any season
                of famine, therefore those people will hunger more
                (which people?
                the natural seedbed of that morality
                is plague, and all such endeavor
                instructs one to move our daughters
                to some green island
                in the sea, we are so far from Galilee
The sum of her
shall perish, has begun
to perish in the darkside
in the prescribed field of misery
and she will hardly avoid the destruction
of her nature,
a material of birth
as a car of new life
    not new, novel, the life
    is older than that we know as prima materia
        And soon when there is no need
for waitresses, or telephones, doctors' wives

and automobilists, they wither
on their still green vine, no more tears
to water life, no more varicose veins
the Kaddish will be said
not as a formal memory
but for the working of a curse, venus
will be likewise a disease transmitted for a secure experience
a memory of Eve for some isolated engineer
who said if I don't do it, someone else will
    A man,
    in that framed condition
    of some totally onanized culture, who will
    transmit with the bills of requisition
    the bill that held Leda off the ground
    in that throbbing moment when she saw histories of the future
    in the bright feathers, knew the spines of
    that ancient creature in her thighs

  the engineer's note:
Send me a little syphilis this month,
                    I have been reading
                      some old books
and in that sense
there is no loss to *a* man
of his earlier knowledge,
a yawn simply defines the brink of availability:
                Hello there Ed, congratulations!
                I've forgotten the *de*tails
                but it sounded *fabulous*!

It is the night of the opening
of the new art-grocerystore and all the shoppers
were discussing theology, a science which has no subject-matter,
something about the indistinguishability of environment where all
the mistakes of logic create a different object, something
without tears, something
                as I get it less like
                the terrestrial entry a cave or
                less similar volcano than woman
                something omitting holes
                a specifically anti metaphorical being
                like a man protruding, an extension
                no intention, space is still not conceived
                (as surrounding: infinity is the inability

                    to conceive, the collapse
                    of surrounding,
                    female principle was structure
                    before and somewhat after the opening
                    of the art-grocerystore
So tears, or the rose enfolds
the moisture of its passion
the girl my daughter, 14 today
and such eyes, all interior, a proud thing
born in 1951, not yet bestowed with any curse, she is
Chansonette, a woman, hopefully, for nomads
a principle older than man, a running out
the tear dropped into an earth rapidly drying tonight,
the disappearance instant
into the most unimaginable laundromat, the danger
a wholly adjectival father might worry over
in the nest of the most corrupted notion thus far: America!
of how men might, if they were noble
behave in their last moments we barely speak
except for the relatively sour hope that some nineteenth century
and romantically singular form of bloodletting
be reinstated because the man in the street hears a choir
of pioneers' voices and thinks of brigadiers when a rightist is hurt
where he sits on the porch of his finca faraway

                                        or of how we might
plead our case in the face of Sartre's observation
that this is a nation where those who care
are the damned of the earth, *running* I will add
before the furious nations who snap at our heels
with a momentum of the centuries, and I stand
behind the pane at my window one of those hopeless men, some silly
                                                        toscanini
leading the symphony
in the street, directing the movements, I do so know
all the scores by heart, by a memory
saturated with defeat, where crisis and alienation
are no more new than any other condition but were always
bred in this strewn and used land, no cultural tricks of assimilation
to form a cover,

                    bunchgrass is an isolated cover,
has a slight brief flower,
and I can tell my daughter no secret.

A LETTER, IN THE MEANTIME, NOT TO BE MAILED,
TONIGHT

The arm swings
and the tracery
of its arc is
of the same breed
of immense
              emotion
     as the horizon on a blue morning
Art wounded in this theocracy
          we can no longer be held together
     by the mere terms
     the mere conditions
     of our captivity
the arrow of the art passes through our centers
and it used to leave us amazed at the rapport
of our mutual singular disaffection.
                              In this Theocracy
headed by the texan in buckled shoes
and the popart grin and surrounded by women
with all those funny embarrassing names we saw men murdered
and maimed on TV, and waited to hear the smug explanations
and shouted our derisive punctuations while the picture
and the voice played on played on and later went downstairs
into the parlor of that lame Wittgensteinian and tried
on his defective record player to hear Snooks Eaglin.
Thus we practiced assiduously and mutually an extension
of that Art
designed by more apt men than we were then
to keep us apart but more than that, to keep
our senses apart, to make dormant at least
and at best to make wrecked
to have made inoperative the mechanism
                                   whereby we track
with the capturing powers of our own love
the expanding universe, as it goes
in our brief time beyond us, as we reach
the black dot in our eyes, for that largeness
the interruption of nothing else could matter,

                                    Let's take it
from another letter: To be agitated *is* to be involved
in this Theocracy where the *Structure* has rotted —
no Bible state and not that scheme which anyone
might understand to get in or out of, and
it is nerves it all goes to, the language does not help
because there is too much slack from that to its source
the reference to the first real utterance, nerves is
precisely what is left of God
                                    as State

I agree with everybody in this cold longitude. Everyone
is right, ripe that word means, this evening is as
false as that evening we spent in wyoming with the man
we went to see, and who else, of *all* people to all
places could have beckoned us thither save him, of Buffalo
and that air so dry in the eye of its wetness and infertile
to an extreme we almost drunk ourselves to death with
who because he could not otherwise explain left
                                    the next day
and took all the gods with him
                                    however
this letter is to a black man from whom I have become separated
in a newest of all land with the oldest hyphen of the western world
hot wet rooms where everyone ages rapidly, and we said pragmatic
goodbyes,
            a tension of action which all things become in forlorn places
where some outcast people find a place at last and others wander
with an open and unplaceable heart in this most enforced of all
                                    wildernesses.

INAUGURATION POEM #2

1

Behind all the trees in America there are men standing
and they are spooks, they are the men, and the women,
and the children who look around, past the dirty protective bark
hiding the filth of our days here, the cover
of what we have done with a rope and a knife and a chair and chamber
on crossroads at night, in the apertures of alleys, in the backs
of restaurants, on mesas with broadbrimmed former athlete
and presently cowboylooking, or, the boy in the vocational program
today will be the sheriff and the petty hood, his equipotential
tomorrow, the cover of what we have done. Everyone knows our benevolence
but not everyone knows our benevolence was always well grounded
in a base of return, not gain, for God's sake, that
was never enough, but return, wall street is no miss named
it does separate, it does wall our gigantic society off
it marks us apart from where we are, I don't mean it as
a joke, Ah uz not jokin, mah boy married a heebrew, do they
let them heebrews go onto the sahara desert or are they only arabs
there? But they are Spooks.
Spooks is not a misnomer. Indians are spooks too.
Lovers are spooks and communists are spooks in america
like Trotsky is a spook in mexico, only Rightists are real
thus their blood must be let so they can be spooks too
so they can be americans too, because if you aren't a spook
you are *not* an american. Poets are spooks.
Negro poets are the spookiest biggers.
Buggers are Biggers.
The Bigger the better? Oh my. The University of Alabama football team
they take the sperm of a universe they want to deny
into their open uptilted mouths every time they play, it drips
whether he knows it or not
across the white pearly acres of the quarterback's teeth,
that is the field he truly plays upon, there is where
those signals are called.
                    And so,

upon this cold January day,
in a heated box of glass, here I am without a coat on, the trees
have been sprayed with a chemical which is the private property
of a local Washington tree-sprayer, to keep the feet
of starlings off the branches

above, the spectators, as if the starlings wanted to attend that badly
or gave a shit, carry 20 dollar bills in their beaks, and sit
on the seats below. Sheriff Rainey could come if he wanted
on a bus eating popcorn, but the starlings, who were *invited*
several decades ago to this hemisphere will get the hot-foot
no hot-dogs, suggestively enough, and in-spite-of-all baseball
into the mouths of the southerners who ride the fronts of busses.

Next time, don't marry a jew, and don't hire the man with the beard
and don't bring niggers to hoe your cheapshit cotton, but for that
matter don't get some bespeckled idiot from new england to set blades
so seeds can be &c, you will always find that those people black
or white, will breed like hell once they get jobs, and get those spicks
out of Imperial and places like St. Paul minnesota, and Laguna california
How could 190 million Americans have been so thick fingered!

Those are the troubles simply put —

                                   OH Mr. Johnson
when you take your war on poverty to Inez Kentucky,
to the tarpaper shacks, don't look into every face, don't shake every hand,
don't look ahead to a bright highway of hope
for the impoverished and unemployed of the nation, please
pass some laws so the 8 to 12 thousand-a-year (those excluded are unintentioned
pinhead can pinch the ass off his colleague and build cabins
near hemingway's grave in ketchum in peace

                                   and when you mount the rude
steps of the cabin of Tom Fletcher take your secret service men with you
so they may spit and fume on his unwashed presence, let them tell him
because they know, he's a little, unimportant man, let them watch him,
his every poor, defeated, loser's, hopeless move, loser, buried
in verbiage. Surrounded by wadding, his sons

                                   need
a college education, they know better, they know he needs a bath.

                                   Don't
say anything to him, jobless,
who earned 400 dollars last year scratching for coal on the surface
of neighboring hills, you in a neatly pressed business suit and he Tom Fletcher
in khaki trousers and tattered sport shirt a gust of wind knocking over
the privy door, in ten minutes of chatting, mrs. johnson engrossed
in talk, slop on the floor, neat of course, the poor are always said to be
neater than anyone else, poor but honest, or that age-old bullshit about
mended clothes, if they are neat and clean being as good as, if not better
than the clothes of the rich whom you OH AMERICANS
stand before. Take care of yourselves, said Johnson, as he left the hillside cabin
and don't you forget now, I want you to put those boys through school.

2

Americans, you were that stupid from the beginning the rest of the world
stood with their lower jaws dead with amazement at you, and you never
never did get that the point from the beginning, Columbus, Cabot,
Nuñez, LaSalle, Estevanico, the Kid, was mystic, was precisely non-
rational, you really thought you had to annihilate the Narraganset
which means people of the small point, oh god, the moon, is the body
of the small point, your whole concern is of small point, the war
saw concerto seems to your crossed eyes a song of great emotion
But you missed it, they made no images; their divinities
were ghosts; they were extreme spiritualists. Plenty of gods
The Sunn
   Moone,
     Fire,

Water,
  Earth,
    The Deere,
      the Beare,
        &c
And &c is the most important gods you missed. For they
were the Manitous, they dwell in you at different times.

            If they choose.

3

Augury

The blood does not flow from a red vein
as Lawrence through Cooper had it,
and it does not flow from a pale, beautiful
white vein, as Wyndham Lewis had it, and it does not
flow from a black vein as Malcolm X would
have it, the blood does not flow at all.
The land is stained, and it is true
it is stained black, because black is active,
red, the first color of that stain, before black
has washed out and sunk into the ground
and now comes up secret, inward, resistance
where Lawrence was perceptive,
and the white parades, Sousa, where Lewis
with his pale mystic articulation was perceptive

being blind to the throb of black,
but it is all stain, not flow,
black has a gloss, black must have white
black dies without white, Mao is too asiatic
and pure, he can not see across
either the largest land or the largest
water mass he is surrounded by, purity is
his world, business, the chinese business man,
the chinese gambler, the chinese fucker, they
do it, quickly, many many offspring, mass
mass the morass of being working blending, mass
they have no stain, america is stain, the stain
of the west, black and white will blend, obscure
the edge, we shall all fuck that edge away eventually
we so desire each other, the red is oriental, lost
in his most recent place, black and white are the new
comerado — enemies hanging together in every room
in every gutter and A-bomb site every cheap hotel
every penthouse, in the mines on the plains and in
the pumping heart-cornfields of america, every thing
in america is american to a virus, blood spilling
the german blood will not spill, nor the pole
nor the mexican, not italian, not the old previously spilled
no one white kind with the black
                         RED
              will return
                                   to the East, via the west
        on a landbridge rebuilt
                          past Diomedes
where they will run cattle or spanish horses across siberia
the last of the primitive people in the world

          who can go home

WEST OF MOAB

The caravan wound. Past the pinto bean capitol
of the world and mesa verde.
Bitterly cold were the nights.
The journeymen slept in the lots of filling stations
and there were the interrupting lights
of semis all night long as those beasts
crept past or drew up to rest their motors
or roared on.

A modern group in cars.
They travelled north at an angle
and the tired engines whirred
moreso the rear plant of the nazi car
from the strain of the great
american desert. Past places
they went, like only mormons
and in Green River
they had coffee and talked to an old woman
whose inconsistency was radical
so demented was she
by the isolation of the spot and the terrible dry winds
that blow down upon south Utah.
and what she had to ward them off
were not the slow dreams of indians
but a pool table and a rack of cold sandwiches.

The beer was cold
The four sat and drank.
Hot, the climate was tolerable only
within the confines of bars or on
the open stretches of road at mad speed
or at night when the bitter cold sat over the southern
Colorado cliffs.

In the bitterness of the great desert
they tried to get comfortable in car seats.
Utterly left behind was
a mixed past, of friends and a comfortable house.

They felt sorry for themselves perhaps
for no real reason, there had never
been in their baggage more than a few stars
and a couple of moons, you've seen their surfaces
in pictures.
They came finally to the brick facade
of salt lake & much beyond. A year later
those who remained celebrated —
almost as an afterthought, and remembered
that day it snowed when they left,
September 1st . . . now it is October
and winter has not yet sent her punitive expedition.
Warm days. It is afternoon. The leaves
come and go in the Alberta wind sliding down
across our country
and they sit still facing the north slopes
of the mountains, the remnant of a Southern Idea
in their minds.

IDAHO OUT

For Hettie and Roi

"The thing to be known is the natural
landscape. It becomes known through
the totality of its forms"
                                        Carl O. Sauer

1

Since 1925 there are now no
negative areas he has ignored
the poles have been strung for our time together
and his hand is in the air as well

areal is hopefully Ariel

    So black & red simplot fertilizer smoke

drifts its excremental way
down the bottle of our
valley
toward the narrowing
end

coming into the portneuf gap
where its base aspects . . .
a large cork could be placed
but which proceeding from inkom

        or toward

past the low rooves
of sheep's sheds the slope
gains rough brusque edges
and you are in it more quickly
than its known forms allow

    or the approach from
the contrary side of the valley
there is a total journal
with the eyes
and the full gap stands

as the grand gate from our
place
to utah bad lands and
thus down
to those sullen valleys
of men who have apparently
accepted all of the vital
factor of their time
not including humanity.

And not to go too far with them
they were the first white flour makers

they jealously
keep that form and turn the sides
of the citizens' hills into square documents
of their timid endeavor. The only
hard thing they had was first massacre
and then brickwork
not propaedeutic to a life of grand design
wherein *all* men fit
but something
for all its pleasure of built surface
and logic of substances as
the appeal of habitat
for salt lake downtown is
not ugly,
but to a life of petty retreat
before such small concourses
as smoking, drinking, and other less
obvious but
justly necessary bodily needs
not including breeding which in their hands
is purposive.

From this valley
there is no leaving by laterals.
Even george goodhart,
a conventional man, as all
good hearts are
knew, with a horse
and access crosswise
to creekheads
the starving indian women could be fed
with surplus deer.

Who was the pioneer boy who died in a rest home
and was a new local, i.e.,
there is implied evidence
he never heard the cry of the pawnee
in his territory.
Which, it is said in the human
ecology term
is to be a hick, howsoever travelled. And
while we are at it it is best said here:

The mark of the pre-communication
westerner
travelled in local segments
along a line of time
utterly sequestered
thus his stupidity required the services
of at least one of his saddle bags
and, in the meantime
his indian friends
signalled one another over his head
as he passed on his businesslike way
in the depressions
between them, in long shadows
they looking deaf and dumb, moving fingers
on the slight rounds
of nebraskan hills.

Of a verge

of the land North
and an afternoon is no good
there is the width of the funnel rim
and sad people for all their smiles
do scurry and sing across its mouth
and there are no archipelagoes of real laughter

in alameda
and no really wild people save stiff
inhibited criminals.

So when gay youth was yours
in those other smaller towns on the peneplain
of central america and the jerseys
the white legs of girls stand truly by stoplights
and Edward Hopper truly did stop painting
all those years. But we stray
we strays, as we always do
and those mercies always wanted

an endless price, our jazz came
from the same hip shops we walked past
the truly, is no sense speaking of universes,
hanging from that hook

       I had in mind the sweet shop
something so simple as main street
and I'll be around.

But I was escorting you out of Pocatello,
sort of north.
Perhaps past that physiographic
menace the arco desert and
what's there
of the leakage of newclear seance

           to Lemhi
again a mormon nomenclature
where plaques to the journey of Lewis & Clark
but the rises across the too
tilted floors of that corridor
at high point the birch
and then toward North Fork
you must take that
other drainage where yes
the opposites are so sheer
and the fineness of what growth
there is that lifting
           following
of line, the forever bush
and its thin colored sentinelling
of those streams
         as North Fork comes on
on the banks of the magnificent salmon
we come smack up on a marvelous beauty from Chi.

Who has
a creaky cheap pooltable
to pass the winter with
and the innocent loudmouthed handsome
boys who inhabit the
winter there. The remarkably quiet winter
there,
all alone where the salmon forks.
It is so far away but never long ago.
You may be sure Hudson.
And
She said
shaking her dark hair
she used to work at arco
and knew the fastest way
from salmon to idaho falls —
you may be sure
and in a car

                or anywhere,

she was a walking invitation
to a lovely party
her body was that tactile to the eye
or what I meant
she is part
of the morphology
the last distant place of idaho north,
already in effect Montana.
Thus, roughly free,
to bring in relative terms.
Her husband, though it
makes no difference,
had sideburns, wore
a kind of abstract spats
wore loose modern beltless pants
and moved with that accord to the earth
I deal with
but only the heavy people
are with.
    They are "the pragmatic 'and'
the always unequated remnant"

2

My desire is to be
a classical poet
my gods have been men . . .
and women.
I renew my demand
that presidents and chairmen everywhere
be removed to a quarantine outside the earth
somewhere,
as we travel northward. My
peculiar route is across
the lost trail pass past
in the dark draws somewhere
my north fork beauty's husband's
dammed up small dribbling creek

fetching a promising lake (she showed
me the pictures) a too good to be true
scheme she explained to me,
to draw fishermen with hats on
from everywhere
they wanted to come from.
One of the few ventures I've
given my blessing . . . she
would look nice rich.

3

We were hauling . . .
furniture. To Missoula.
We stopped in the biting
star lit air often to have
a beer and to stretch our legs.

My son rode with me
and was delighted that a state
so civilized as Montana
could exist, where the people,
and no matter how small
the town,
and how disconnected in
the mountain trails,
could be so welcoming to a lad,

far from the prescribed ages
of idaho where they chase that
young population out, into
the frosty air. There is
an incredible but true fear
of the trespassing there of such
patently harmless people aged 13.

But not to go too much into
that ethnic shit, because
this is geographic business,
already, in the bitteroot
there sat snow on the tallest
peaks and that moisture factor
caused trees now gliding by
from one minor drainage
to another until we came
to the great bitteroot
proper and the cotton woods
and feather honey locusts
lining its rushing edges.
Once, when I was going the other way
in august,
a lemhi rancher
told me the soil content
of the bitteroot was of
such a makeup that the cows
got skinnier whereas
in the lemhi, you know
the rest, although of course
the lemhi is dry. It's
like a boring popular song
all by himself he'd love
to rest his weary head
on somebody else's shoulder
as he grows older.

    From Florence to Missoula
is a very pragmatic distance
And florence is the singularity
Montana has, one is so drunk
by that time. Fort Benton,
to your right, across stretches
of the cuts of the Blackfoot, through
Bowman's Corner, no

the sky

       is not

bigger in Montana. When
for instance you come
from Williston
there seems at the border a change
but it is only because man has
built a tavern there
and proclaims himself of service
at a point in time, very much,
and space is continuous from Superior
to Kalispel. And indeed

That is what the dirtiest
of human proportions are built on
service by men there before you

could have possibly come
and you never can.

But if men can live in Moab
that itself is proof nature
is on the run and seeding very badly
and that environmentalism, old word,
is truly dead.

4

So he goes anywhere apparently
anywhere and space is muddied
with his tracks
for ore he is only after,
after ore.
He is the most regretful factor
in a too miniscule cosmic
the universe it turns out your neighbors are

The least obnoxious of all
the radiating circles bring
grossnesses
that are of the strength of bad dreams.

5

Let me remind you we were in Florence
Montana.
Where the Bitteroot is thick
past Hamilton, a farm machinery
nexus
for all that unnutritious hay
and in florence we stop.

Everyone gets out of the trucks
and stretching & yawning moves
through the biting still starlit night
a night covered with jewels
and the trucks' radiators begin
to creak and snap in their cooling off.

We shiver. Each limbjoint
creaks and shudders and we talk
in chatters of the past road, of the failing
head lights on the mountain road — and in
we go.

　　　　A wildly built girl
brushes past us
as we enter. Inside
it is light, a funny disinherited place
of concrete block. The fat woman
bartender,
has an easy smile as we head for the fireplace
in the rear and as we go by the box is putting out
some rock and twist, and on the table
by the fireplace there are canned things, string beans
and corn, and she brings us the beer.

Florence. It is hardly a place.
To twist it, it is a wide spot
in the valley. The air is cold. The fire
burns into our backs while we sit on the hearth.
The girl of the not quite
believable frame
returns, and her boyfriend is pulled
by the vertically rhythmic tips of her fingers
reluctantly off the stool,
but he can't

he, the conservative under riding buttress
of our planet can't, he has been drinking beer
while she, too young for a public place
has been pulling a bottle apart in the car.

So there you are. She is
as ripe and bursting as that
biblical pomegranate.
She bleeds spore in her
undetachable black pants
and, not to make it seem too good
or even too remote
or too unlikely near
she has that
kind of generous smile
offset by a daring and hostile look
again, I must insist, her hair
was black, the color of hostile sex
the lightest people, for all
their odd beauty,
are a losing game.

. . . I can't leave her.
Her mother was with her.
She, in the tavern, in Florence
was ready,
with all her jukeboxbody
and her trips to the car
to the bottle.
There are many starry nights thus occupied
while the planet, indifferent, rattles on
like the boxcars on its skin
and when moments like that transpire
they with all good hope begin again somewhere
She made many trips to the car that night . . .
an unmatchable showoff
with her eyes
and other accomplishments.

6

And onward
bless us, there are no eyes
in Missoula, only things, the new
bridge across Clark Fork
there is civilization again,
a mahogany bar
                    and tickertape

baseball, and the men are men,
but there are no eyes
in Missoula
like in little orphan annie and is?
the sky bigger there?

        The sky disdains
to be thus associated and treacherous cowboys
who drive cars live there.
Say the purity of blue over Houston
that unwholesome place
is prettier
and the graininess over Michoacan is moodier
and I have been to wyoming.

7

The trip back sadly as all trips
back are
            dull
and I did
see the old bartender woman of florence
this time in her restaurant part 50 yards
away from the tavern between which
she ran apparently with the speed
of some sort of stout gazelle
but not the broad with the fabulatory build.
She that day was probably off in an office somewhere.
Pity daytime lives.

But everyone was tired. We had unloaded
the furniture, early the next morning
and before the bite of the sun quelled the bite
of the stars we left, going the long, time consuming
way
south. Sober business.
The Beauty of North Fork was there as she will be
till she dies sometime
(and by the way she runs a tavern)
Thence to salmon and across the narrow bridge
and out
into the lemhi. I say
if it weren't for the distances
and for the trees & creeks I would
go mad, o yes, land, that one forces
a secondary interest in, vanishes
as a force as you drive onward.
This is only obvious.
This is only some of the times we spend.
You go through it as though it were
a planet of cotton wadding . . . and love
its parts as you do the parts of a woman
whose relations with earth are more established
than your own.

But of physical entirety
there is no need to elaborate, one has
one's foot
on the ground, which is the saying
of all common and communicable pleasures
and my arm around your shoulder is the proof of that.
But I am ashamed of my country
that, not as areal reality, but as act
it shames me to be a citizen in
the land where I grew up. The very air chills
your bones, the very ungraciousness of its replies
and the pressures of its not replying
embarrass my presence here. God knows
we do what we can to live.
But the intimidations thrown at us
in the spurious forms they have learned truth
can take, in a time which should have been
plenty and engaging of the best that each man,
if he were encouraged to be even that, and
not slapped in the face as stupid, cut off

from all other peoples to make him hygienic of
views not viable to this soil, which is no more
sacred I tell you than any other the earth
has to offer, for she in her roundness has kept
an accord with her movements great time has not yet
seen aberrant. Mice crawling on a moving body?
can they, may they really offset great movement?

The very air,
if you are awake, can chill your bones
and there is little enough of beauty
finally scratched for. It is not
the end pursuit of my countrymen
that they be great
in a great line of men.
An occasional woman, won't,
though I wish she could,
justify a continent. In the parliaments
of miniscule places she is there
and gives them substance,
as in Florence, and North Fork
for she was gracious as leaders
are now not and I begin to believe after all
these years there *is* an aristocracy
of place and event and person
and as I sit here above this valley
I sought to involve you with
and take you out on a trip
that had no point, there remains Montana
        and it is nice. But not infallible.
The sky is a hoax.
And was meant,
once suggested,
to catch your eye. The eye
can be arbitrary,
but its subject matter cannot.
Thus the beauty of some women.
And from Williston
along the grand missourian length
of the upper plains you go, then the Milk
to Havre
that incredible distance once along a route
all those clamorous men
took . . . they now grow things there not horticultural
only storageable, things of less importance

than fur
for furs then were never stockpiled, it would
hurt the hair,
                        that Astor,
he'd never have done it.

And yes Fort Benton is lovely
and quiet, I would gladly give it as a gift
to a friend, and with pride, a place of marked
indolence, where the river closes, a gift
of marked indifference, if it were mine.
If the broad grass park were mine
between the river and the town
and to the quick rise behind.
And then up to the median altitude of Montana
Sugar beets and sheep and cattle.

Where the normal far
are the stretches of Wyoming
and north Dakota, Idaho
is cut
by an elbow
of mountain that swings
down, thus she is
cut off by geologies she says
I'm sure
are natural
but it is truly the West
as no other place,
ruined by an ambition and religion
cut, by a cowboy use of her nearly virgin self

            unannealed
by a real placement
                        this,

this
is the birthplace
of Mr. Pound
and Hemingway in his own mouth
chose to put a shotgun.

SIX VIEWS FROM THE SAME WINDOW OF
THE NORTHSIDE GROCERY
(for Helene on Washington's birthday)

1

Saturday afternoon. The hill is a reminder
with its slope of a counterpart outside
Sedro Wolley — wooded second growth there
snow and the black scars of juniper here.
The glass shines with the land beyond
red freight cars and the vast house of shops.

2

We occupy red enameled chairs
in the backroom, drink beer and eat greek
cheese and olives, white salt of the cheese
black salt of the shrivelled olive spit
into the ash tray. Beyond the old pink front
the red green stripes of the awning sway in the breeze
of these last days of February. All the panes
remarkable of clarity, an uncle sam kite
writhes up from the hands of the black boy
the rattle of its paper cannot be heard.

3

Goat cheese and greek olives. The owner
is sullen and friendly, he calls the black women sister
they come and go inside his grocery, one thing at a time
it does not pretend to be a small supermarket.
Cold air, clean glass. We rest and watch.
The occasion for this excursion is in the selected strings
of a life gone terribly goddamn lonely. It will be a march.
A frail cloud moves with silence into the window.
No sound in the store. No bell on the door.

4

The dark children fly their kite —
we share a common exile — they run
I stay here in the woven light
of a backroom.
It is pointless to make verse of this fibre. I could write
all the names of my absent friends
on the window in black
and the light would grow less
and then lesser
and I would sit motionless
on the dark side of my thought
I would sit in the deep shade of my yearning
I would have supplied me the proper nouns
of my darkness.

5

And my lady looks from the same window, over
one yard altogether away, another picture
of the world, white house isolated, a lost railroad
building, this vast change rung with the same air
and we are, by the same air, a rest of those
measures of wood, of the same kite, cans bounded
by trash she has in her view, and poles
of loosely hung wire, some power lost altogether
back of the glass as the trembling portrait
of uncle sam, of all the continuing weirdness
in the ennui of the falling sun, and I stare at her
and her lips part very little, slow and pleasantly
vagrant talk, the measures are the stillnesses
made various by the code of friends' names, those nouns
drop like greek olives from our fingers, and the pits
are in a real way the crashing verbs of
a mistaken local rapport. Be patient
and give me your hand, there is something of a beginning
everywhere, this is a new part of town.

6

There is a part of the world over your shoulder
can't be seen in a window and can't be pulled
through the holes in one's eyes yet a fixture
of some boundaries is a small cure haphazardly grasped
or torn loose from a confused day, a tiresomeness
arrived with a permanent smile hand outstretched
I love you now more than ever and stand waving my arms
at the edge of the swarm of self breeding considerations
to say it, the mailbox, that post, is sought out
by both of us a triangulation of what we share
as elsewhere,
it is a twin exile, the small town's portion
of futility, the self mockery with an interchangeable tire
that makes us dare what we are. Thus a window
is that seemingly clear opening our tested knowledges
pass through and the world shakes not at all
before the weight of our disappointments, you will
and would be part of the new hemisphere
until it dies of the same old loosely wrought manifestoes.
All those sounds from the broken washing machine
are trying to tell you something sweetheart don't laugh
one day it will speak and not stop
all things have an insistence of their own.

DAFFODIL SONG

The horns of yellow

    on this plain resound
and the twist on the air
of their brilliance
              Say where
say where I will find
a love
    or an arabesque
of such rash fortune.

SONG

my wife is lovely
my children are fair
she puts color on her lips
in front of the mirror
there is stillness everywhere
my hand is on her shoulder
we are leaving the house
the sun is in her hair
and since october
it has grown darker
there is frost in the air
I am unwise
to think of her as there
  those parts of her I adore
are here
the years have gone by
everywhere
now our house is near
alongside other houses
we laugh, sometimes,
sometimes we construct
a single blue tear

LOVE SONG

Captured, her beauty
would not leave her
thus inclined by the railing
she never lifted her head
from the waters
a blue gull drifts
     she moves from the rapture
of the ascending fog.
Lost in the moving passengers
she left the ship
and entered the city.

LOVE SONG

Out of the north branch of the river
out of the foam of it running
runs my desire
so the fish fall never ending
continually forward
and she stays eternally there
and indolent winter stars
are in her eyes
     indolent as she resides
all seasons by the fork
of my desire.

A VAGUE LOVE

The Bannocks stand by the box
they sway to the music.
A California truck driver
in with a load of pianos
shoots pool.

Their women
are not beautiful
they are not

but their eyes
have deep corridors in them
of brown hills of pain and
indecision and under every
lash

is a question no man, not
even their own
can answer.

Where is the *deer?*
That is not the question.

tic tok, stop de clock.
sings Fats Domino.

We all stand swaying.
it's someone's turn to shoot.

ANOTHER VAGUE LOVE

Down 5th it is cold
yes the dry air is filled
with pieces of dust
they cut the eye as would a file.

Driven along, every day
toward center
this is a town
of vague love

And what you see if you can
is the truth:

SONG

Oh Gods of my disembarked soul this is sad
a merriment of unteachable waywordness
I tell you the gleaming eye
is a mirror of
                the green hills
where love struggles
                        against the drought
in the desert
in the spring
in the quickness
of the fresh bush
        over the cove.

A WILD BLUE, YONDER

Let me say
we had a canary
who rode to Idaho
with Bob Creeley
swinging in a cage
on the seat beside him

Sadly in the last of March
I opened our door
and the bird flew out before me
but that was hours ago

A very nice bird,
liked Syeeda's song flute
and returned always to the cage
to roost, and had taken
to a picture of that man
on our shelf, which we then put
in the window facing out
                              to summon it
Helene saw out the window
a bright blue
bird in the sage
and felt better and
then we gave it up.

IN THE SHADOW

a dim light shines. The city
is reflected on the overcast
when our conveyance comes
in. Late September. Cool.

She rises just another move
in the dark just another
month another moist point
on my dead journey.

Her mouth I never saw
nor the surprise of
her busy limbs, yes her
eyes strayed.

It was late September and
cool air pale shadows held sunset
in their traces.
She left in a car, the dust grew.

SONG

If the world
or a life
or all of this
love,
all the pleasures
we do not sow
and those we do
love,
sometime end.

                  If any of this
end
     we will know
what we knew to begin
a vacancy
of dreams
of costly motion
temporary cities
and our happy faces
where we were determined
as some blunt nosed dog
           permitted exercise
from tree
     to tree
on the public concern

A SONG

There is a blue sky
over the flower, there is
a green sea beneath
yet there is no bliss
along my way now. . .

In the casual flight of this day
there is a yellow flower edged
in blue
there is a sky filled with snow
and along my way there few bright calls
of spring, there is hardly a chance
there are ahead no tricks
to turn a season, all friends
are sober.

I have a dark blue sky
inside my head, ah,
there is a flower here
and there, and yes, believe
I'll miss this time, sometime,
these old cold mountains
these cold blue hills
sometime.

THE EXPLANATION

There was a dark interior
where I waited and there
were dark odors dark music. All my days
pressed flat, float
off
in the breeze.

The sky over the southern arc is leaden,
rain, falling or not
running in the gutters
or not, is rare here.

We left with dexterity but desperation
a place we could no longer abide
and all explanations now seem
unfit, unfit.
The long sought ease

a hand on a curved hip
was part of other lives
and offered no explanation and got
a ready stare
                    so falteringly
to the wall I went
and they said My My
and shook their heads.

CHRONICLE

It is January 12
and midwinter, the great dipper
stands on its handle in the sky
over pocatello.
The air, a presence
around the body when I go out
the door to relieve myself
is well below zero.

Yes it is well below.
This land is well
below, say shoot it, longitude
and latitude, yet it stings
like the Yukon, and standing,
to get back to that,
I thumb my nose several times
at the city below, it is midnight
and the lights are stationary
through the cool absent fog.

Inside Fred plays his cello
and that air sings thereby.
I run my fingers through my hair.
Here, all around, is
the world, out
on points, on the horizon are
friends close and far gone.
With the tautness of those
chorded strings bind them
together,
this air will kill us all
ere long.

SONG

So we somewhat stagger together
down the street, heads down
smiling and not smiling
she making her ceaseless prattle
and laughter
           she is the goddess
who leads us after a worried pedestrian
or a hapless dog, and I go
always it's true wrapped in a cloud
a press of obscurity that keeps me
in a small car of priority
a propriety
          of attention
   and not missing any part of it
she is that tactile
on the street,
against my side, taking us
around the circumference of desire

            oh stars be bright!
in the forecast of your grand moments
and when the terror and pestilence
you will surely drive with a stake into my heart
is there
let us have been
for a while
          in a superior conjunction
          back of the sun.

SONG

Christ of the sparrows Help me!
  the soot falls
      along the street
 into the alleys.
december.

and sometimes
  its rain falls
      along pocatello's streets
  into its alleys
  along its black diesel thruways

There is no far away place
could satisfy
there is no forlorn bird
could outdistance my desire.
When the vacation
of my heart is that complete
the pain of this
particular moment
is unbearable. The sun
strikes my book laden table
my room is my skull
I could have you tell me
this pain behind my eyes will soon be gone
I could listen, I could die
seized by a foolishly contrived misunderstanding

or listlessly watch
      the two single
figures bent
and in the rags of careful hesitation
feel their way along the sidewalk
past my window
old men
leave a city already made lonely
by the outcast words of pointless conversation
  go,
along the intolerably windy highway west of here.

  And mind us
there were no marks of the bruise of friends
there aren't any traces of that turmoil, you stay

as you were, there were
a few headlong pitches onto the ground
a torn shoulder to remember
a few unhappy nights.
drunk with the high necessity to talk
fast and loud in crowded bars
And then, in the street
to spit silently out
the cheap guilt
and all the casual half meant and self aware
inward chastisement
a petty reward for myself, like saving a nickel
and insisting even with a smile
it was *my* life I lived
the suspicious terror I'd turned around
too many times to keep track
I said you said I said You said I said.

PARLOR CAR BEER

They look coach, in the morning
pants wrinkled.
And I *am* coach, CHICAGO spelled out
across my front teeth.
Don't want to be sleeper.

   They
look sleeper
coming in from the other end, the
dirty & tired
have a beer
with the rested & clean.

   Get this:
we talked of the all England
ice skating championships, 1959

   How
some skills pass the understanding
of the uninitiated
right in the middle of Nebraska

53

POEM IN FIVE PARTS

1

Van goghs boats
sat on the beach
as I sit here
good lord as I sit here

and van goghs boats
are upturned
the bows set east
as I do

and the crosspieces
on the masts
they are strung out
as my arms are

oh were I only
red &
white &
blue

and in the distance
more white as
the sails, the
lonely white
triangulars
are

dim-
inishing

how I am
only
as the distance
goes

blue

2

I love you

3

Februaries
are hard to face
there were trees
this winter possessed
of a grace
they are
white bare
siberian elm
around the corner
in the garden
the cold air
this spring —
will be
    changed
    and obscured
deformed
as I will
a growth
of indetermination
while waiting
out the season

4

I have
certain dreams
at midday
and you are their vintner
at eleven I go
for the mail, a card
a misconcordance
of a letter
on missing, a lapse
of two months
the cement is frigid
beneath my bare feet
it is the end of january

5

Where are you
Henry James sits
on the table, an increment
of difficult sentences
the same sun shines
  you left without one thought
of me
without one desire
to let me know
or look back
all at once,
            as if suddenly
you ignored one half year
of mutual consent

I am a casual fool
now
I do so regard
the labor
of my own
            careful
peace of mind.

SONG

This afternoon was unholy, the sky
bright mixed with cloud wrath, I read Yeats,
then black, and their land of heart's desire
where beauty has no ebb
                    decay no flood
but joy is wisdom, time
an endless song
                    I kiss you
and the world begins to fade
I kiss you not, the world is not.
I would not give my soul to you yet
the desire inside me burns.
November. The eighteenth was the coldest
this season, encumbered with routine errands
out past the factory
                    black sulphur
and in the dense checks
of its burdensome smoke the intense yellow tanks,
hooded, there sat a smell of weak death

and we pass these days of our isolation
in our rigidly assigned shelters
heads bent in occupation
a couple of pointless daydreamers
smiles lit and thrown into the breeze,

    how artful can love
suffer in the cross streets of this town
marked simply by the clicking railroad
and scratch of the janitor's broom.

DARK CEILING

Broad black scar the valley is
and sunday is
where
      in the wide arc
 the small lights of homes come on
in that trough.

      Burnish my heart
      with this mark

Furnish my soul with the hope
Far away and by a river
In the darkness of a walnut stand.

There
      is
no home, no back.

All is this wrong key, the lark
sings
      but his voice trails off
in the snow. He has not
brought his meadow.
The starling's
 insolent whistle
is the truth here — dark smoke

drifts in from the morning fertilizer factory
and men there return lamely
to work, their disputes not settled.

THIS MARCH AFTERNOON

Pride kept me away.
                    Her eyes, indelicate
as they were,
were there nonetheless
                    and her eyes guided
me into the recesses of my own
                    untrackable
world, oh goddesses
did I like Harpagus crave a future rule
of this world as over the years I grow older?
A bitter clot of time rides in my throat
and Nay once again the Graces say.

SONG: HEAT

                    Massive time
the pacific controls our continent
but what controls me is far
less in size than that and far
more burning, oh heat

a continent is my forge
buried deep in the caloric inside
is our relative, the fire
          the twin bellows of love
                    cavity of the chest
in the mountain the door
on the lips the red explosion
in the valley the unlit incubator
   sperm of politics flow
                    a river
in the ocean of the edges
basins catch us
in the mystic of the spray the return
onto the land again
          the spore of politics
the ringing arrangement of love

THE RECEPTION

I am not amused by
your speech
don't grate my ear
with thin brilliance.

And stop spitting peanuts
into my drink
as you say you adore
poetry.

The new script of
the rising internationalism
of which you are a part
shall forward itself on
artificial cognizance

while the old ignorances
having been forgotten by you
will remain as a smoldering
ash
to consume you in future
esoteric studies and evaluations
beyond your reach.

In that time when all
have moved off
and the new debts
are payable, the new mortgages due
a sizeable population
will know
as a huge parent

attention! Kill them!

then when the new drifts
have set
as usual upon the old —
unmelted

you with your tears will be
bewildered no more then
than now, a simpering preliminary
to peace, russia and america
dated bigleaguers, the baldheaded
men in your stands will crush
their popcorn bags with elation.

Of advice
I would give you none.
Hot August 1962
the beautiful double menace
of the gorgons rest
at the edge of each mesa

though the one mortal one
of that triumvirate
has been killed
          she the most beautiful
mass has killed you
none of you can be the other two
with their tongues out
the mighty
and the wide wandering.

The Arco desert, humanity,
might be Phlegra. Do not
accept the helmet which makes
men invisible.

SONG: WE SHALL REFRAIN FROM THEM

On the shore of our world
there appeared one day
an unhappy coincidence
of natures born but not meant
for each other. An infernal compliment.

And no more
was said. No more intended.
There is bred a dark hurt, an intersection
far smaller than time
too brief to exist in space
of a luminosity only
far redder than the red flash
of the tongue
of Eve's keen snake
now we are at the tranquil pass in our mountains
all we had expected, all we had
made secure
is routine. The cool valley beyond
is filled with cabbages of persons
in rows to the end of time
their heads are fixed
and it is not that they can't see Icarus
rise in his superb ambition
but they will not, they will not see

Our Gods
trap and they slay
they pretend to know nothing of frivolity
while their whole pleasure is instruction
in that quality.

But they have no gods at all to play with
they have invented *one*, a dull number
and they wave small flags of angry color
in one shrivelled hand, on one stunted arm.

THE SMUG NEVER SILENT GUNS OF THE ENEMY

Their muzzles are at the door.
Did you see them, did he
see them, minutemen
rising out of the silos
A winter wonderland of
the white busy north.
The smug guns, trained on
The whites of their eyes
are grey
         and disputations
of more guns come
into the ear:
    The manipulated price of sugar
    The death of great ladies
    "I'll shoot my second if you'll shoot yours"
    Concentrated insecticides
    (flow like milk in the river
    You will be greeted
    on the outskirts of town
    with a vegetable brush
    and tips on good living
    An interview with a turkey farmer
        (gobbling in the background
the news that Bertrand Russell
    is a sick old fool
    The seminar ends when the squat madeyed colonel
    announces the way to peace thru war and shoots the moderator

And more corrupted reports follow you out
the door, they implore you to think young
and you do
it is such a pleasure in the sagebrush
in the open saturated air
zipping up your pants
having made more of the latest news
on the new snow.

FORT HALL OBITUARY: A NOTE

A drinking party
(no war party)

Sunday morning
they drank solax
containing methyl. . .

Fort Hall Indian Police
found Reeta Poonee, 37
dead inside a shack.

Bigbear passed out
in a car
outside the door

they were all watched closely.

(Bigbear taken Bannock County jail
warrant charging disorderliness
checked regularly

But when Deputy John Gouge checked at 7:20 a.m.
there was no more Bigbear . . .

and thus,
Coroner Justin Juice said
No goddamn autopsy heah into this
heah death! Ah am satisfied they died
from drinkin.

and Reeta
and Bigbear

are

MOURNING LETTER, MARCH 29, 1963

No hesitation
    would stay me
from weeping this morning
for the miners of Hazard Kentucky.
     The mine owners'
extortionary skulls
whose eyes are diamonds don't float
down the rivers, as they should,
of the flood

    The miners, cold
starved, driven from work, in
their homes float though and float
on the ribbed ships of their frail
bodies,

    Oh, go letter,
keep my own misery close to theirs
associate me with no other honor.

EUGENE DELACROIX SAYS

dated Valmont 10-16
october 1849
the common people
will always be
the majority

they make a mistake
in thinking
that great estates
are useless

But furthermore he says
It is the poor
who benefit most by them

And the profits gained do not
impoverish the rich who
let, them,
take advantage of the little
to be sure
windfalls
which they find on their estates.

Now let us begin again this morning.
The poor.
And the middle class
or anyone might
fence off their approaches
necessity is a naturally
more separable thing
than poverty.
In this case the poor were
allowed to gather fuel
on the estates, given them that right
by the republican, fear that word,
government.

Much as today the man bent between the tracks
in Appalachia east kentucky
his malnourished and unemployed fingers
articulating very small pieces of coal indeed
and his children grimly beautiful

because their eyes have been made large
as witnesses
as the lean roll of years and owners
stripped the hills of their former
mountain glamour.
                    Bent in the dim light
of that specific cabin space they had,
those unlucky children, a meal
of various cereal dumped on the market
to make room for vaster crops next year
a thing they couldn't have understood
or that charity is quite often
a device to prevent spoilage,

                              nor were they
ever allowed to consider that the merely farinaceous
will not support the life
of a carnivor. But this is just
the bestiality of the major euphemism
of our day, supplementation.
Retrained they may become garage mechanics
and press the temptation
of match cover education
between their fingers
the rest of their days here in the western hemisphere.
Now, if a fire has to be made
and a supper has to be got, that's not
here nor there, here,
but back of Recife they *wonder* a lot of the time
in Kentucky they do not
in all of Hazard county they do not.
And it is an inevitability that one day
those ugly eyes prolix with beefsteak will be
snatched out, and south america
will have been all along much to their amazement
a specific location not to have been misused
and kentucky will have been a noun
that smouldered like a burning mine
and, I have to add, I hope those satraps
do not wake in time.

SONG: VENCEREMOS

(for latin america
(for préman sotomayor

And there will be fresh children once more
in planalto and matto grosso
green mansions for their houses
along the orinoco
    take away the oil
    it is not to anoint their heads
    take away the cannon
    and the saber from the paunch belly
    overlaid with crossed colors
    those quaint waddling men
    are the leaden dead toys
                 only their
          own
        children
          caress
    while the great eyed children
    far away in the mountains, out of Quito
    pass thru the crisp evening streets
    of earth towns, where they caress
    the earth, a substance of *majority*
    including the lead of established
    forces,
who can do nothing
    but give us the measures of pain
        which now define us

Take away the boats from the bananas
they are there for the double purpose
to quell insurrection first
and next to make of an equatorial food
a clanging and numerical register in chicago
this is not industrial comment,
it is not Sandburg's chicago
not how ugly a city you did make
but whitman's fine generosity I want
a specific measure of respect returned for the hand
and the back that bears away the stalk
as a boy, in illinois

peeled away, in amazement, the yellow, brown lined case
thicker place
when the arced phenomenon
was first put in his hand
a suggestion and a food, combustion!
keep your fingers from the coffee bush.

Nor,
on the meseta Basáltica, or back in town
in Paso de Indios
can the people be permitted
the luxurious image of Peron
and his duly wedded saint
they can be taught to deny
the dictator and his call girl
in the sports car
hide themselves in some corrupt
rooming house country
with a blue coast
and damned clergy

"memory, mind, and will
: politics
"there are men with ideas
who effect"

Force those men.
be keen to pass beyond all known use
use the grain on a common mountain
for those who are hungry
treat hunger
as a ceremony
be quick to pass by condition
and the persuasion of mere number
teach the parrot, who rises
in the sunset
a cloud
to sing,
destroy
all talking parrots
I ask you
make for the
altar
of your imaginations

      some sign   Keep
the small clerks of God from your precinct
be not a world, and therefore halt
before the incursions of general infection
              from a stronger world,
    dance,
              and in your side stepping
    the spirit
        will tell where.

DWARFING WITH CHEMICALS:
A PROMISING AGRICULTURAL TECHNIQUE

Chrysanthemums
are too tall
       plant two
in the middle
attractively
compact.
They all look like Orville
Freeman
some of them like General Walker

Ultimatums for all
living matter, the distinctions

are used only
to tell you it can't happen here.

THE SENSE COMES OVER ME,
AND THE WANING LIGHT OF MAN
BY THE 1ST NATIONAL BANK

My stepfather stood on the corner
by the national bank, quiet

                  the hot lights
nights moved on
between those week periods
              the old men
spat, they seemed possessed of stronger points
a willingness to jut from their foreheads
not articulation but a world of determination and only
that, an insistence, a manifestation of the bottom jaw
then, as now, the most stupidly local preoccupation,
                              you think
this is abstract,
                nigger no, don't
and there weren't. Not there, of course, we were
                        alone
and it could be said there were questions unformed
for the lapse of any plausible answer, the walnut dropped
literally onto the ground in the woods
and rotted there through the year, and the people cried
out in their ineffectual way for white flour and pork,
canned peaches my aunt brought once was a ceremony
                              I almost
waited under the table.
                The afternoons. So Do you
think to think of love? Or weld
that affair
              with the heat of ancient transplanted tassels,
the relief of mystically rough elements
                      The dead watch
of the sun,
the unyielding severity of a farmer feeding pigs
the routine collection of mud
mixed with the sharp green smell of excrement on their boots
old times gone over
                save us
from the anterooms of the moral what
the shiftless which everyone wore, blue jackets

overalls, an unspoken sign in the starch, laundry
was very much, as now, a form of calculation, land
                                        and starch,
this is no judgement, this is
the weight of dissimilar things bound together
by a strictly regulated common deprivation
the low and the high, no middle, held in a smiling equilibrium
you may eat only the shit I give you. One could not
comprehend. . . Under a mulberry tree the road was purple
with their running from their farms into town. Passing
at night on the black road in the car I marked the passing
over those spots under those boughs. It meant nothing, it
could mean nothing, one would not have mentioned it. Abandoned
the trees were like my youth. It was a stain of assurance
I preferred to the cant on the bank steps but an utterly sad
and contemptible inability to insist on the stain of reality
and a woe of that lowly order became my sign and weight in that land.

            I became that land and wandered out of it.
Sharp
        and keen with the fever
this thrill of spring in the Lord's prayer
which I carried and still love as a vague solace
I carry, confused
                    that ceaseless speculation over
the ways of love
into the darker borders
of my wounded middle years,
                            a practical self-pity

            There was a girl
            who was a resolution
            with whom I walked the empty streets
            and climbed the watertower for one night
            to show myself, she standing a white spot of summer
            on the ground, and looked out I did
            over the lights of a realm I thought grander than
            and any of it, altogether, was very little, and when
            the pictographic scratches in the silver paint told me
            as I walked around
            the cat-walk expression of what had happened in the 1930's
            men vomiting from hunger
            on the thin sidewalk below, a lonely mason
            with his business ring on, but beyond,
            in the little shoe repair shops the men,

part of a hopeless vigilante, exhaling the slow mustard gas
of World War I. My mother, moving slowly in a grim kitchen
and my stepfather moving slowly down the green rows of corn
these are my unruined and damned hieroglyphs.
                                                    Because they form
the message of men stooping down
in my native land, and father an entire conglomerate
of need and wasted vision. All the children
were taught the pledge of Allegiance, and the land was pledged
to private use, the walnut dropped in the autumn on the ground
green, and lay black in the dead grass in the spring.

        there they do lie, the principle
residue of my past, and the past
of my gutless generation, nineteen year olds
invaded the white house today, a screen
was put up to shield the nervous exit
of Ladybird, they sang and refused to move,
she split and I felt it possible again
at the end of a very long winter
to be a less schizophrenic american, a little
of the pus was spooned out of my brain, I gave
an arbitrary grade to a backward black girl
I remembered to spit on the sidewalk
when I thought of the first 35 hundred marines
who landed in Vietnam yesterday. I spoke of
President Johnson as the logical extension of
Increase Mather, my heart, like theirs,
a "civit box of sin" and late in the afternoon
explained *Metamorphosis*, and Kafka as a product
of a hung-up family, and a hung up people,
bringing forward, inching nearer
the perpetuality of the lives we lead on the edge
of the great american desert where you certainly
do not
want to be buried but buried you are, the horizons
recede before you, they are busy with the presentations,
that remote we are, of the tilting planes of escape
. . . which are :   the speculation of what we might do,
        an *imagination* of the geometry
        of our location
        the problem of the potato
        stamped to identify its place of origin,
        that, for one of the poorest of foods

No one,
has loved the west I came into, this is not
a Shulamite maiden, nor does anyone care to whisper
this far into our ear, the allegory does not exist, the marriage
will not come who would marry Simplot or Anaconda
I warn you world of good intention the birth of Mohammed
will be fought in this neck of the cut-off world
devoid of the culture that spawned it consciously
and moved on, any new blood will
turn to an unnumberable plasma
we could still walk into the banks
and demand the money, but the usual sadness
— we have been preceded by cosa nostra, there is
nothing so lame and halt as lateness

SONG: RITUAL PARTY IN AN ALLEY

The young teach
    the young.
      in almost *all*
almost all
      societies
    the old men teach
  and the novice is put under
      a blanket
      afraid to look
      while the old men around the fire
         prepare
    the sheathblade
    a stone before steel
    and before stone
    they rent off
        with their teeth
    the pubertal cover
    the blanket of the phallus

    thus ushered toward the majority
    a new sheath of clay for the penis wound
    (in the States that means drink

      and drink, the young
    are drunk into it, deserted

  the young teach
    themselves, no poultice for the wound
      they are obviously
      inturned, in spite
    their whistles
    are so tuned
    into broods

    they go into broods
    always one, always many
    to be left at the edge
    with the old men

to join the ranks
of the old men, every one of them
too late, in their blue suits

the medicine dirt of the earth
showered from them
their world is ugly
with infection

A LUXURIOUS JUNGLE IN WHICH

They are the police
        the flowers
in a deep jungle too rife to transgress
        the bars, believe me, grow
  as any vegetation, look say the substantial voices
of any place and you do, the details of our terror
are that
distracting
                because it is your game they
seek to persuade you to play,
the irony Hawthorne caught
        the large mystic gesture Melville made
inside an utter disregard and disdain
for the local.

The flowers grow in jail. The penetration
of light, the atmosphere of possibility,
and don't call that abstract, call that a man and woman
hanging their heads by a single artery, call that what
the thread of life is, not what instead it might be
call that garden History, do not call it eden
an allegorical tale based on certain unlikely presumptions.

SONG : EUROPA

Red wine will flow
sadly past your lips, and leave
with fullness their parting
october is orange
with desolation
the mountains are abandoned
each winter sunset
to those cruel marks of red
or whole lines of remote ranges
lit of desire for you as they recede
                              toward oregon

Nothing will happen.
The brutality of your frankness
has come to me
inches at a time,
and so slowly the pain marches
through the veins of my soul
with the heavy step of a migrating herd
tramping out the vintage
Evening is
              that closing part
of you I sometimes hum as a song to myself
looking down the street through my fingers
through the wreath of myrtle
                        with which you have embellished
                                  my horns

I call
with the thick weight
in my throat
over your terrain
                    O she is a small settlement, there
she is an atmosphere
and we are above it all
under her white gown
                    and against my bare shoulder
snow flakes fall
        a slight scent of ginger
  fresh in the wind
of our trip to Knossos

FOR THE NEW UNION DEAD IN ALABAMA

The Rose of Sharon
     I lost in the tortured night
  of this banished place
   the phrase
    and the rose
    from wandering
away, down the lanes
   in all their abstract directions
   a worry about the peninsula
  of the east,
      and the grim territories
        of the west
       here in the raw greed
     of the frontier my soul can find
   no well of clear water
     it is pressed
  as a layer
    between unreadable concerns,
      a true sandwich, a true
    grave, like a performance
      in an utterly removed theater
    is a grave, the unreachable action makes
    a crypt
       of distance,
   a rose of immense beauty
     to yearn for,
          the cutting of it
      cutting off the world
     the thorn however
   remains, in the desert
    of american life, the thorn
  in the throat of our national hypocrisy
    strewn we are along all the pathways
of our exclusively gelding mentality
     our gelding spirit
      we stride in
       our gelding culture,
   oh rose
      of priceless beauty
    refrain from our shores
   suffocate the thin isthmus
    of our mean land,
 cast us back
  into isolation